CONTENTS

1

THE AUTHOR

CHRISTABEL BURNISTON M.B.E., National Froebel Diploma (1st class) L.R.A.M. (Speech and Drama) A.L.A.M. (Speech and Drama) F.R.S.A. G.O.D.A. F.E.S.B. President of the English Speaking Board, has done pioneer work in the field of oral communication in various parts of the English-speaking world. In addition to examining for E.S.B. in every kind of educational establishment, her many former appointments include external examining in spoken English and drama to the Education Institutes of the Universities of Aberdeen, Cambridge, Durham, Leicester, Newcastle and Nottingham. She is well-known as a lecturer, examiner and adjudicator. Her educational tours abroad include: Australia; New Zealand; Poland; U.S.A.; Canada; South Africa; Zimbabwe; Sweden; Malta; Hong Kong.

Founded the English Speaking Board 1953.

Founder Member of the Women of the Year Association.

Member of the Society of Women Writers. (Council Member 1992).

PUBLICATIONS include:

Speech for life (Pergamon Press 1966; reprinted in Australia 1975)

Creative Oral Assessment: its scope and stimulus (Pergamon 1968)

Spoken English in Further Education (Methuen 1966 republished 1974 E.S.B. as Spoken English in Advanced Education)

Anthology of Spoken Verse and Prose, Part I and II: Johnson, Burniston, Byrne (O.U.P.) 1963

Speech in Practice: speech and exercises for Seniors (E.S.B.) 16th printing 1983

Speaking with a Purpose: a speech course for adults (E.S.B. 9th printing 1983)

Rhymes with Reasons: Burniston and Bell (E.S.B. 14th printing 1979)

Into the Life of Things: an exploration in language through verbal dynamics: Burniston and Bell (E.S.B. 1972; 1977)

Creative Oral Assessment: a handbook for teachers and examiners of Oral Skills (E.S.B. 1982, 1983)

Direct Speech with Dr. John Parry (2 years course for G.C.S.E. and A level) Hodder & Stoughton 1986.

Life in a Liberty Bodice: random recollections of a Yorkshire childhood (Highgate Publications 1991).

Sounding Out Your Voice & Speech (ESB 2nd printing 1992).

ACKNOWLEDGEMENT
   The author wishes to thank the many teachers and tutors who have been generous with their appreciation and suggestions. Special thanks to many E.S.B. colleagues especially Jocelyn Bell for her wise counsel and patient proofing and for the teachers and students who used Speech in Practice and Speaking with a Purpose to the 16th printing.

AUTHOR'S NOTE

This book is an amalgam and a revision of my former books; Speech in Practice and Speaking with a Purpose. The former originated in 1955 and was finally re-printed in its sixteenth edition in 1983. The latter, first published in 1961, was finally published in its ninth edition in 1983. Thousands of students of speech and drama, now mature actors, teachers and theatre directors or caring parents still pay tribute to the help they got from these pocket editions.

Even so my intention was to drop them both, as being over-used and out of date, but as hundreds of orders emerged and followed the out-of-print notice I overcame my reluctance and surprised myself by becoming enthusiastic about this extended publication.

Part 1 deals with good talk in a variety of small and large group situations, implicitly stressing the importance of good listening.

Part 2 includes a range of definitions and rhymes for vowel and consonant formations including the neutral vowel; variety of pace and rhythms and the flexibility of English cadences.

The vowel exercises and vowel chart exemplify received pronunciation without imposing its acceptance. Only when we can recognise and reproduce the accepted 'norm', (R.P.) can we appreciate the characteristic and varied deviations or dialects and regional speech.

In using this book students should select exercises and refer to the vowel chart to help their personal linguistic needs and should not feel that the book is a sequential course of study.

CHRISTABEL BURNISTON

FOREWORD –

'Speech in Practice' and 'Speaking with a Purpose' have for many years been a positive byword for teachers and students of speech and drama. This new book, like the books it supersedes, helps students to have a firm basis from which to explore and develop speech skills.

The simple analysis of vowel and consonant formation and classification, in an essentially practical manner, will be enlightening for students of all ages and a variety of needs.

The aim of the book is to foster clear articulation, enunciation, vocal vitality and range; such exercises bring out all that is best in lively regional talk while training the ear and the speech mechanism to recognise, and if appropriate, *use* Received Pronunciation.

All text books are best combined with the skills of a good teacher. This book certainly invites that partnership.

John Wills
Head of Vocal Studies
School of Drama
Welsh College of Music & Drama
Cardiff

PART ONE
SOUNDING OUT YOUR VOICE AND SPEECH

In this practice book of speech in action a large subject is being introduced in a small frame-work. Many of the sections only get as far as the scaffolding from which one hopes students will go on building.

The overall criteria for effective speaking, which this book does not attempt to cover, are:-

- Clear and purposeful thinking

- Growth of vocabulary to make clear thinking possible

- Alert access to this vocabulary

- Fluent association of ideas in verbal terms

- An ability to group words into an accessible and concise grammatical form: Standard English.

- The development of flexible range of vocal tone

- An awareness and feeling for significant rhythm of speech which includes the pointing of key words and the subordination of unimportant syllables and words

- Clarity and precision in enunciation without affectation or aggression

- An acceptable pronunciation, accurate in stress and near enough to 'Received Pronunciation' to cause neither ambiguity nor embarrassment. Received Pronunciation is the kind of spoken English used by radio and television announcers in the European and World Service, English broadcasts. It is no longer the prerogative of 'those born in the south east of England and educated at Public Schools' but a stable style of pronunciation which helps intelligibility and international usage.

- An overall co-ordination of physical and mental response (bodily ease, significant facial expression and gesture) which gives the *listener* a feeling of sincerity, confidence and friendliness.

- Standard English could be described as the kind of English generally accepted as the standard of educated usage for writing and speaking in most situations. Unlike France, Britain has no final authority to arbitrate on whether words are slang, regional, colloquial, or 'standard' but there is an accepted code of grammatical constitution of sentences which, unfortunately, most British schools have failed to teach in the last decades. This has resulted in students being at a disadvantage in speaking and writing their own language and in learning other languages.

SOUNDING OUT YOUR VOICE

The voice of a well-adjusted person will be full- toned without strain or jerkiness and have an easy swing through the many notes of the speech register. Voice-training for speech, therefore, must be psychological not just physiological and it may well be that the first is more important than the second. Therefore, if your voice is to be harmonious and pleasant, create an attitude of mind which is harmonious and pleasant. Negative thinking will either make your voice droop or it will create a harsh defensive tone.

Take the following situations making up your own dialogue and listen to one another not only for meaning in the words themselves but for the meaning in the voice.

1. SINCERITY AND KINDLINESS

a) Say a few informal words of welcome to a new student or employee.

b) You are receiving a visitor to your college (school, factory, hospital, premises). Give the appropriate information.

c) Congratulate a colleague on his or her promotion or successful achievement.

In each of these tests the value will lie in the constructive criticism of the others who listen. They will be able to tell you things about your voice, tone, tone colour and delivery which you had never realised.

2. AUTHORITY

Give the following commands and orders with decision clarity and authority but without anger or aggresion

a) "Miss Jones there are still five letters waiting for replies. Will you come at once to my office, please, and we will finish them so that they can be sent before 6 o'clock to the General Post Office".

b) "Will you please all leave this room in a quiet orderly manner and assemble in the yard outside.

c) "The law in this building is NO SMOKING. Anyone breaking this rule will be dismissed without notice".

d) "Will those who asked for places on the coach returning to Birmingham, please see me in my office at 2 o'clock".

Was there, in each case, no possible doubt that you would be obeyed without question or rancour?

3. SYMPATHY

Now can you extend your range of sympathetic tones. Remember that you must *feel* compassionate. Notice if this is really reflected in your vocal tone.

a)   Say a few words to a friend who has to undergo a serious operation.

b)   You have wrongfully accused a colleague of a serious error. Apologise to him/her.

c)   Say a few words to a colleague who has not been given the expected promotion (award, bursary).

4. PERSUASIVE TALK

a)   Put over some new project to your organisation (or School or College Board of Management or Board of Governors or Executive Committee, Parish or Town Council) which you feel would be beneficial.

b)   You are organising a dance (gala, gymkhana, agricultural show etc.) Explain to your committee how it can be made to pay.

c)   You are having a visiting lecturer to your works (business, school, college, church, factory, hospital). Give a preliminary announcement which will make your colleagues or employees want to attend.

5. MEETING THE SITUATION

Life is considerably smoothed by those who have the confidence and tact to meet all kinds of people and situations without fuss but with a quick perception of what the situation demands.

Try out one of the following every-day incidents with your group:

a)   Introduce a friend from abroad, who is staying with you, to a newly arrived guest.

b)   Introduce a friend to another who is in the same line of training, business, profession or sport.

c)   The telephone goes – the caller is your tutor or Principal or Agent – but you are due to leave to catch a train. Deal with the situation.

Names are important; say them clearly but give a little helpful friendly information about the people you are introducing. If you know any common interests mention them, this gives a subsequent talking point for those who have been introduced. Relax so that your friends and colleagues feel at ease.

BREATHING

If you breathe deeply, rhythmically and easily then be thankful; you may not need special breathing exercises. When some people think consciously about the diaphragm or the intercostal muscles they may create troubles which never existed before.

But it is hardly likely that you *are* breathing perfectly, or, if you are, you may not be using your breath in the most effective economical way for speech.

Useful Exercises

1)   With hands lightly touching the lower ribs, breathe deeply feeling the outward extension of the lower ribs. Check that there is no upward shoulder movement.

2)   Repeat the exercise exhaling on numbers 1 – 5.

3)   Repeat the deep breathing exhaling on a humming note of sustained M sound.

4)   Repeat the deep breathing and exhale on a softly articulated S sound. See how long you can take to complete the exhalation. When you breath control is secure you should be able to do this for 45 seconds without strain.

5)   Repeat the deep breathing and exhale saying:
   a) The days of the week
   b) The months of the year
   c) The alphabet

RELAXATION

This is fundamental in every activity. Watch the first-class golfer or tennis player. The action seems effortless. This is because every muscle not needed for the job is relaxed and every muscle needed for the job is in a state of tonicity not strain. Bodily movement is balanced, rhythmic and powerful. Let the chin rest at any easy right angle to the spine. Avoid any clenching of the teeth. Have a feeling of relaxation in the mouth. Release the jaw bone 'hinge' as much as possible. Lips should touch lightly in moments of repose but behind the lips the teeth should be apart – only then is the jaw relaxed.

≈ ≈ ≈ ≈ ≈ ≈ ≈ ≈ ≈ ≈ ≈ ≈ ≈ ≈ ≈ ≈ ≈ ≈ ≈ ≈

≀ REMEMBER: ≀

≀ We do not need much breath for voice but we need the support of ≀
≀ deeply filled lungs. This is impossible without good stance. Avoid ≀
≀ slumping at the waist; keep shoulders down.   ≀
≀ Good breathing tones up your whole physique and helps to calm
≀ your nerves. Laughter tones up the diaphragm muscles and ≀
≀ contributes in no small measure to relaxation.   ≀

≈ ≈ ≈ ≈ ≈ ≈ ≈ ≈ ≈ ≈ ≈ ≈ ≈ ≈ ≈ ≈ ≈ ≈ ≈ ≈

SHAPING YOUR THOUGHTS WITH ECONOMY OF TIME AND WORDS

Good form or style whether the design is for a ship, a sardine tin, a story, a power-station a powder-case, a poem a play or a novel implies:

a)   fitness for purpose

b)   clarity of line

c)   dignified simplicity

d)   pleasing rhythm

e)   the use of appropriate and durable material

f)   the indefinable quality of individuality

This is true of good talk.

Choose one of the following subjects:

a)	Roses	j)	Photographs	s)	Golf
b)	Clocks	k)	Bibles	t)	Soccer
c)	Stamps	l)	House of Commons	u)	Rugby
d)	Coal	m)	Zip Fasteners	v)	Bowls
e)	Paper	n)	Super markets	w)	Riding
f)	Wine	o)	Theatre	x)	Swimming
g)	Oranges	p)	Cinema	y)	Driving
h)	Bread	q)	Art Exhibition	z)	Skiing
i)	Fans	r)	Tennis		

GIVE INFORMATION on any one of the above in a one minute talk.

When you have finished ask yourself or each other:

a)   Were the words well chosen?

b)   Was the meaning clear?

c)   Were the phrases compact and the language direct?

d)   Had the sentences an easy flow?

e)   Did you use the best words in the best order?

f)   Did it sound like YOU or a text book

g)   Were you at ease and relaxed with your subject and your listeners

Finally, did you entertain and/or instruct your listeners so that they *really* listened and then remembered.

ECONOMY OF LANGUAGE

Good talk is clear, colourful and concise. Usually the shorter or least pretentious of two synonymous words is the better one.

e.g.			
	begin	rather than	commence
	flat	" "	apartment
	lift	" "	elevator
	car	" "	automobile
	jam	" "	preserve
	enough	" "	sufficient
	rich	" "	wealthy
	napkin	" "	serviette
	sofa	" "	settee or couch
	put	" "	place
	sweat	" "	perspiration
	salt and pepper	" "	condiments
	porch	" "	vestibule
	top price	" "	ceiling price
	increase	" "	escalate
	now	" "	at this point in time
	buy	" "	purchase

EXERCISE FOR COMMUNICATION TO A GROUP

Each speaker to *prepare* a one to two-minute talk on one of the following –

1) A prepared summing-up or criticism of any personally selected radio or TV programme.

2) A summing-up of the main news items of the week.

3) A description of a game, a sporting event or theatre performance

4) A description of an important character in the contemporary political, artistic or social scene.

5) An appreciation of a recently read book or play.

6) A description of a new building.

7) A description of a well designed and functional article you have bought (or hope to buy).

Listeners will comment afterwards on the clarity, economy and vitality of the description. Remember there is always time and space for the champagne to bubble. Often less information and more humour would alert your listeners to attention. Time and care in preparation will be needed for these exercises but the speaking time must not exceed *two minutes.*

It is much more challenging to put one's thoughts into words in two minutes than in twenty minutes. As Pascal said 'I have written you a long letter because I had not time to write you a short one'.

CONVERSATION AND DISCUSSION

Conversation, at its highest level, is an art using man's supreme intellectual powers: his knowledge, wit, human understanding and good humour. For the masses it has rarely been anything more than a factual or utilitarian means of communication, though many country folk still are spell-binders in their exchange of stories.

In ordinary life, conversation is a friendly shuttle-service of kindly enquiry and response which helps to ease human relationships. In this relaxed conversation (to change the metaphor) one person creates a chain with an open link on which the other person can hang something; thus in the end a continuous chain is created from the associated ideas of the conversants. We begin with 'small talk' which we hope develops into genuine sharing of ideas and experiences.

SUBJECTS FOR INFORMAL CONVERSATION AND DISCUSSION
with a group of 3-5 people.

1) Your pet superstitions.

2) Television: a stimulus, a danger or a soporific.

3) Trade Unions: a necessary power or a pest.

4) What would you do if you won £50,000?

5) Personal 'hates' in modern architecture.

6) Sunday newspapers.

7) People you enjoy hearing and seeing.

8) Crowd behaviour in sports.

9) What do you mean when you say a person is educated?

10) What would you do if you knew you had only one year to live?

11) Tell a story against yourself.

12) What I could do without in life. (Keep this conversation light-hearted and humorous).

≈ ≈

REMEMBER

In conversation or informal discussion that you are also a *listener*.
Throw the ball into the court of one who has had little to say.
Respond to and encourage each member of your group by eye contact, genuine listening and picking up of cue.

≈ ≈

TALKS ON FORMAL OCCASIONS

1. INTRODUCING A SPEAKER

Before attempting this make quite sure you know the person's name accurately. General remarks such as 'well-known-to-you-all' break down when, in fact, it is obvious that the introducer knows nothing about the speaker. See that you are up-to-date on his achievements., Far too often the 'Introducer' snatches a printed or written potted biography and gives the qualifications and early days which the speaker has now left far behind. Remember that the best and most brilliant speaker is still grateful for a 'build-up' and the nervous speaker really needs one. Let the talk be short and to the point; 2-3 minutes should cover the salient points and 4 minutes should be the maximum time. Remember, too, that you not only introduce the speaker but you have the responsibility of creating a happy receptive and responsive audience.

2. VOTE OF THANKS

Address your thanks to the speaker and not to the audience. Make reference to points in the address which have specially delighted you. Particular references as well as general appreciation show that the speech is not a mechanical previously prepared one but a spontaneous response to what you have heard *today*. What you have to say, of course, is important but a relaxed happy gracious manner will convey more than hundreds of words.

3. AFTER LUNCH, DINNER OR WEDDING BREAKFAST ADDRESS

This is probably the most difficult speech to make and yet given the right company and the right speaker it is the most fun of all.

Remember that however important the occasion or the group, the guests are in no mood to think or probe deeply. They expect to be entertained. This does not mean cracking one joke after another like eggs in a bowl but rather creating a well-shaped and homogeneous soufflé which rises, as it were, 'above the dish'. Avoid cliches, platitudes, 'you've-all-heard-the-story' phrases (because they have, you know) not too many 'that-reminds-me —' because if it is associated in your theme it will come in flexibly and inevitably.

Remember in all talks, speeches and addresses the vivid graphic example is remembered. Long heavy abstract sentences, however accurate or erudite, are often forgotten by the time the speech has laboured to its close. Go through your speech and strip it of pretentious phrases. Be able to discriminate between sincere sentiment and sugary sentimentality. Do not patronise your audience nor on the other hand play for easy laughs with jokes in questionable taste.

Above all: keep it short! Remember that the shorter the time of a speech the longer you may have to work on it.

It is not possible in this book to cover such a vast subject, the recommended bibliography at the end of the book will be a helpful guide.

General points to remember:

1) Have clear mental bridges from one section of your address to another. A personal 'gimmick' may occur to you of associated words or even initials of a key word. This reduces note headings to a minimum and leaves you free to talk but ensures that you will never omit important sections or wander away from the central theme.

2) Do not be an 'on-and-off-er' of glasses. If you have printed your note headings in your own writing without your glasses you can read them without your glasses; then use your glasses for deliberate readings only.

3) Plan to finish your talk within the time allotted with a sentence that has a sense of conclusion but not door-closing finality. Leave the audience feeling that you could go on and on talking. If they, in turn, feel that they could go on and on listening then you have succeeded.

SELF-PRESENTATION FOR ALL THESE FORMAL OCCASIONS

Remember that they eye is greedier than the ear. 'Listeners' are very often easily distracted into being only 'lookers'. Therefore be groomed but at ease in your clothes; poised not tense or strained; relaxed but not sagging; reposed but not inert; vital but not restless. Let gesture be used easily and rhythmically, not as a conscious added embellishment but as an integrated part of harmonious transmission. Your mannerisms may be endearing (but distracting!) on the other hand they may easily be irritating or maddening. In any case your 'lookers' will have occupied themselves with the 'manner' and not the 'matter' of what you have to say if gesture is fussy and lacking significance.

On the other hand a great personality can have expansive and often outrageous gestures because the mind and body both have stature. The clenched fist of a lesser man thumping on the table or the aggressive arm-thrust of a would-be dictator will not disguise that fact that he is trying to say with his hands something that his mind is incapable of putting into quiet logical words. (e.g. many trade union and political speakers.)

5. YOU AS A READER

Good reading makes great demands on any of us, as it includes many different skills. The newscasters on TV and radio, have, in a sense, been training themselves for their jobs all their lives; they still have to go on preparing and practising every day so that their work is efficiently done.

Reading aloud is a challenge to the intelligence and a test of background knowledge. It measures your ease with words, your enjoyment of them; your co-ordination of eye, brain and speech muscles and the capacity to sense your listeners' response. Reading aloud is an adult accomplishment, quite different from the 'learning-to-read and being heard' in your early years.

It is an effort which brings immediate rewards: the absorbed attention and delight of your listeners. They know and you know, without any 'marking' whether you have 'got across' or not and whether you have been able to communicate so that what you read is *received* and *remembered* by the audience.

All through life you will be trying, through various speech situations, to 'get across' to your listeners in personal and professional relationships, perhaps in clubs, churches, societies and unions. You may not have to read aloud very much, but this practice will help to give you the skill and confidence to communicate your own ideas and to hold the attention of the audience.

With experience of reading aloud your silent reading will be helped to become a rich, imaginative experience because you will see and hear the script transformed into sights and sounds.

But accepting a challenge means accepting its conditions too. To ensure good reading aloud:

a)   Be familiar with your text.

b)   Share the story, poem or play with significant pauses.

c)   Understand that the written text is a blueprint, like a musical score waiting for interpretation.

d)   Realise that the finished product depends on the interpreter

e)   Accept that hearing the words is not enough for your listeners; your vocal range and tone and eyes will communicate meaning too.

FACING YOUR LISTENERS

Stand tall with your weight on both feet. This gives you more power in your voice and breath support. Your listeners, too, feel that you have more confidence and authority.

Your eyes should go ahead and scan the whole phrase or sentence. Dialogue very often precedes the 'signal' word which tells you how to say the words: 'shouted', 'screamed', 'yelled', 'whispered', 'commanded', etc. So your eyes must go ahead to discover the signal word before you say the dialogue.

You will need pauses for reflection and your listeners will need pauses for reception. In this way you share the message with them.

Your voice should create the different characters and atmosphere, and be projected in such a way that every single listener receives your message and remembers it.

The way you change pace from bottom gear to top gear will change the atmosphere and the scene. The story must happen now and it must move away from the printed page.

WINNING AN AUDIENCE

Choose an exciting paragraph from a book you have thoroughly enjoyed. Work on it until you can transmit that enjoyment to your group. Introduce the book and the author clearly and give a persuasive enthusiastic comment on your choice, before actually reading it aloud. The test of your success will be how many of your listeners want to borrow the book for reading.

Remember that generally speaking, you will need twice the time for reading aloud than you will need for silent reading.

ASSESSING YOUR PERFORMANCE

Give yourself a thorough check-up before meeting your listeners. Are you making the best of yourself? Ask yourself:

a)   Do I fully understand the passage and the words?

b)   Have I grouped the words into complete thoughts?

c)   Have I discovered pauses, other than commas and full stops?

d)   How have I emphasised necessary points, making the text come alive?

   with:- change of volume; pace; eye contact; tone; facial expession

e)   If there are different characters in the reading, do they *sound* different?

f)   Will the listeners remember what I have read?

6. THE INTERVIEW.

PRESENTING YOURSELF

Your written application or C.V. will give details of special achievements, courses, skills and examinations. The point of the personal interview is to find out the following:

a)   your attitude to people and work

b)   your practical common sense

c)   your manner and ability to work with and for a team

d)   your enthusiasm

e)   your sincerity

f)   your energy

g)   your voice and speech (not accent so much as clarity and vitality)

h)   your reliability

i)   your adaptability

j)   your conscientiousness

k)   your willingness to learn

Arrive punctually. Give yourself a few minutes in which to relax and take in your new surroundings. If you feel nervous, sit back in your chair, breathe deeply and interest yourself in people and things around you. You can learn much by your observation.

Wear clothes in which you feel comfortable but not sloppy. If they are outlandish or too new you will be consciously thinking of your 'effect' instead of listening and responding.

Employers or heads of training departments are usually busy people and have only a short time in which to get to know you, so give full answers when you are spoken to. They will want to know why you are interested in this particular job or training.

Don't rush your answers. You will be more convincing if you think first and are not merely glib.

Obviously most of the questioning will be done by your prospective employer, careers officer, selection panel, personnel manager or theatre director, but remember that you can ask questions too.If you want more specific details – e.g. the nature of the job, the training, or the person to whom you are responsible – then ask.

7. PREPARING AND PRESENTING YOURSELF FOR AN AUDITION FOR DRAMA SCHOOL; THEATRE; TV OR RADIO.

This is a different process from interviews for a business or commercial world. Theatre, TV, Radio directors or casting panels are looking for individuality; originality heightened imaginative powers but also for adaptability, self-discipline; enthusiasm and controlled energy.

Auditions can prove to be painful experiences since your talents may not be appropriate for the part or parts in question. But however much you are rejected if you believe in your talents, and you are determined, then you will pump confidence back into your deflated ego.

SOUNDING OUT YOUR VOICE AND SPEECH FOR DRAMA

The audition pieces which you have been asked to study and present will be short in print – length but will give scope for interpretative bodily movement and significant pause. Study the whole play before working on the extract so that you get the characterisation in context.

- Don't hold up pace with stresses on unimportant words or syllables.

- Go for the key words and the essential meaning so that sound and sense create a compulsive rhythm of natural delivery.

- Relax every muscle not needed for the job but keep all others in a state of 'tonicity'.

- Know how to be still and hold attention with your eyes.

- Use your head and chest resonators to amplify tone.

- Practise increasing volume without straining the larynx or the throat muscles.

- Practise speaking the quietest pianissimos ensuring that vocal tone and enunciation carry in a large hall or theatre. However such externalisation and projection are inappropriate for the microphone and the camera where 'internalisation' is the key factor.

HERE ARE A FEW PRACTICAL POINTS TO HELP YOU TO COPE WITH AN AUDITION

- Wear practical casual but neat clothes in which you can move freely and feel confident

- Keep your hair away from your eyes — let them be *seen*

- Be prepared for an acted and spoken improvisation or a quick study reading. In this exercise show your powers of concentration in significant pause and eye focus.

- Theatre directors are not wanting to hear pieces of over repeated elocution, they want to be convinced that you are the creator of the thoughts and words and that you are not 'print or teacher bound.' If you have really made the character and words your own then the interpretation will be 'true' from your toes to your finger tips.

8. DEBATING

In controlled debate, there are prescribed techniques and formalities which make the occasion more of an intellectual exercise than a spontaneous expression of opinion. Your college or society may run a debating society or conduct mock elections; if you are to take part effectively you will need to know the order of procedure and the thinking processes which are necessary for logical presentation of your facts.

All debates have a theme presented in the form of a positive statement, called the 'motion', which begins with: 'That' for example:

Motion:

- 'That plays attributed to Shakespeare were not written by him'
- 'That a year of community service should be obligatory between the ages of 16 and 20'
- 'That the rating system should be more fairly spread to include all wage-earners'
- 'That bicycles should be taxed and registered'
- 'That grant-aid should be equal for all 16+ students of whatever ability.
- 'That identity cards should be compulsory for football supporters'

Having decided on the motion, two or three main speakers should be chosen to represent each side of the argument: the 'pros' and 'cons'. They should then do their homework and research to prepare opening statements in collaboration with the other members of the chosen team. Although a debate is more worthwhile if the speakers really believe in what they are saying and speak with conviction, it is a useful intellectual exercise to have to speak on the other side, acting as 'devil's advocate'.

GENERAL ATTITUDE AND MANNER IN DEBATE. Keep alert. Have paper and pencil for reminder notes; keep calm; be good-tempered and occasionally humorous; be sincere but not too intense. Give yourself pauses in which to reflect, to be received, to emphasise and relax. Make eye to eye contact with your listeners. Don't read-talk. Make a few firm convincing points rather than a number of weak ones and try to have a forceful word at the end of each statement.

1. ORDER OF PROCEDURE

a) For every debate there is a Chairman who calls on the original speaker to present the motion and argue in its favour for an agreed length of time. Most societies arrange a definite time (e.g. five minutes, but ten minutes would be a maximum allotment).

b) The original speaker may call on a member of his team (or in the second or third round a speaker from the floor) to support the motion.

c) The opposition follows the same procedure.

d) After equal opportunities for both sides have been given by the Chairman, he then calls on –

e) The original speaker to have the final say and to reiterate his support of the motion.

f) The Chairman then sums up and the motion is put to the vote with 'Ayes' and 'Nos' or with a show of hands:
'All those in favour of the motion please say "Aye" (or show hands)'
'All those against the motion, please say "No" (or a show of hands).

Note that it is human nature to enjoy shouting but the word 'No' has more carrying power than 'Aye' so it might be as well to check with a show of hands.

2. PREPARATION BEFORE THE DEBATE

a) Collect your material under two headings: facts and opinions. In both cases be able to support your facts and opinions with your source. If it is purely your own opinion, say so: 'In my opinion ... ' but if you have also an authoritative source too, then add it to your own.

b) Check that your facts are:
1) clear; short and taut; use graphic words;
2) reliable; check your sources;
3) relevant; keep to the point;
4) valid; give a source or support which makes it an unarguable truth.

c) Check your opinions:

Are they first hand? If they are second-hand give your source.

Explain the authority on which the opinion is based.

Give clear reasons for holding this opinion yourself; quote your own experience.

Give time for your points to be received.

3. PRESENTING YOUR ARGUMENT

Reasoning: your argument must be reasonable, topical and persuasive. Generally speaking there are two ways of reasoning: either by deduction or induction.

a) Deduction is reasoning from the general to the particular. Look out because you can lose the point with blanket generalisations.

It might be possible to say: 'All cyclists are road users, it is estimated that there are ... of them. If each one should contribute £5 to the cost of road maintenance this would bring in ...'

b) Induction is reasoning from the particular case to the general: 'I know an old lady in my street living alone on a pension who was attacked by a violent youth. She had no means of calling for help and subsequently died. There are hundreds of old ladies in this plight. I appeal to you to support this motion which will ensure that simple alarms are installed in every home where the elderly are living on their own'.

c) Rhetorical questions: – powerful reasoning and persuasion can stem from the rhetorical question which is thrown out to the listeners but which is not answered:

– 'Who are these "top people" who qualify for these huge salaries?'

– 'Do people of such high esteem and competence need to be bribed?'

– 'What does the marriage statues ensure? Marital bliss? Protection of children? Financial equality?'

The rhetorical question is useful because you can cause your opponent's points to be put in doubt: if, for example, you were against the road tax for cyclists you could challenge with a rhetorical question: 'Has the speaker for this motion worked out the methods and cost of collecting this tax? Would it not cost more to get in than it would produce?'

d) Reasoning by analogy – In this case you take a comparison and bring it down in your favour. If, for example, you were for the motion on the road tax for cyclists, you could cite a country where this is in operation and quote the income produced from the tax.

Be on the look-out for weak argument on the opposing side: If statistics are quoted are they from a reliable source and if so are they relevant to the present argument?

Notice if the argument is just appealing to the emotions or is an exaggerated sweeping statement: e.g. in the cycle tax motion – 'Well it's a rotten country that takes money from kids', or 'That will mean our newspapers won't be delivered'.

CONTENTS

Part Two

PART TWO

VARIETY OF INFLECTION

(and its consequent effect on the rhythm to point meaning)

Take each of the following sentences and repeat them with different nuances of inflection and stress to give the meanings indicated in a, b, c, etc. Listen attentively for fine points of significance in compound inflection: 2, 3 or 4 notes in one syllable. The phrases a-h are not, of course, spoken.

1. I've just bought a new pair of shoes for Timothy.
    a) as well as you
    b) only half an hour ago
    c) I haven't borrowed them
    d) not second-hand
    e) not gloves
    f) not for Nicholas

2. Uncle Charles might be driving with us to Henley.
    a) not cousin Charles
    b) not Uncle George
    c) it is doubtful
    d) he normally goes by train
    e) not by himself
    f) instead of with his family
    g) but he'll return by himself
    h) but not to Ascot

3. The wedding breakfast will be at 11 o'clock on Thursday at the Royal Hotel.
    a) not an ordinary breakfast
    b) not the marriage service
    c) it is now confirmed
    d) not 2 o'clock
    e) not Wednesday
    f) not the Grand Hotel
    g) not the Royal Restaurant

4. Will you dine with us at home on Christmas Eve?
    a) can you make up your mind?
    b) the rest of your family has already been invited somewhere else
    c) not lunch
    d) instead of us dining with you (2 main stresses here)
    e) instead of going to an hotel
    f) instead of New Year's Eve
    g) not Christmas night

Notice that greater emphasis is achieved by stressing one word rather than several, but the whole speech tune changes to support this nuance of meaning.

COMPULSIVE RHYTHM

Drawing attention to a single word usually calls for a reciprocal 'throw-away' of the other words. But they are not neglected, they are dismissed quickly and lightly on a speech tune which exactly gives the fine shade of meaning. Notice in this respect the rhythmic importance of the *neutral vowel* and compound inflection.

a)   George came.

b)   It was George who came.

c)   It was George who came not Edward.

d)   But you don't seem to understand it was George who came not Edward.

e)   But you don't seem to understand it was George who came to the office not Edward.

f)   But you don't seem to understand what I'm trying to say; it was George, who came to the office not Edward.

g)   But you don't seem to understand what I'm trying to say to you, it was George, my brother-in-law who came to the office not Edward.

h)   But you don't seem to understand what I'm trying to say to you, it was George, my brother-in-law who lives in London, who came to the office not Edward.

i)   But you don't seem to understand what I'm trying to say to you, it was George, my brother-in-law who lives in London, who came to the solicitor's office this morning not my cousin Edward.

j)   But you don't seem to understand what I'm trying to say to you, it was George, my brother-in-law who lives in London, who came to the solicitor's office this morning, not my cousin Edward who lives in Brighton.

Always the compulsive rhythm leads to the main stress *George*. The more phrases that are added the more demi-semi-quavers are introduced. After all this verbiage all you will have proved is sentence a): **George came.** So don't bore your listeners by speaking with a succession of crotchets.

We started with a sentence of 2 words and the last has 40. The last should not take 20 times as long to say but 7 or 8 times as long as the first. This exercise is especially valuable for drama students.

RHYTHMIC FLOW OF PHRASE

Read and read again the following extract by Joseph Conrad from his novel 'Youth'.

'And these were the men. I sat up suddenly. A wave of movement passed through the crowd from end to end, passed along the heads, swayed the bodies, ran along the jetty like a ripple on the water, like a breath of wind on a field – and all was still again. I see it now – the wide sweep of the bay, the glittering sands, the wealth of green infinite and varied, the sea blue like the sea of a dream, the crowd of attentive faces, the blaze of vivid colour – the water reflecting it all, the curve of the shore, the jetty, the high-sterned outlandish craft floating still, and the three boats with the tired men from the West sleeping, unconscious of the land and the people and of the violence of sunshine. They slept thrown across the thwarts, curled on bottom-boards, in the careless attitudes of death. The head of the old skipper leaning back in the stern of the long boat, had fallen on his breast, and he looked as though he would never wake'.

Notice how it starts slowly and with pauses. Bring out in your reading the change of rhythm on: 'A wave ...' and notice how this ebb and flow of the wave shows in the pulsation of the following phrases. The pressure peaks are on 'passed' 'swayed' 'ran' etc. The words too have onomatopoeic values, a suggestion of 'dynamic onomatopoeia' where the movement as well as the sense is conveyed by the sound. Keep all these clauses surging and suspended until the whole sentence is complete to 'still again'.

Examine in detail the following words as you enunciate them and consider what contribution they make in their particular context:

wave, sway, jetty, ripple, breath of wind on a field, wide sweep of the bay, glittering (notice the sharp 'edges' of light in this word) blaze, curve of the shore, violence of sunshine, curled, careless.

Go through the passage again and notice the musical phrasing, how the longer clauses do not necessarily take longer time to say but run swiftly using demi-semi-quaver and semi-quaver values.

Notice too how volume rises and falls. In the two long sentences there is an arc of crescendo and decrescendo. The decrescendo of volume and pace continues in the third and fourth sentences to the quiet stillness of 'as though he would never wake'.

≈ ≈ ≈ ≈ ≈ ≈ ≈ ≈ ≈ ≈ ≈ ≈ ≈ ≈ ≈ ≈ ≈ ≈ ≈ ≈
≬ REMEMBER   ≬
≬ That if you are interpreting a dramatic script it must sound as if it has   ≬
≬ never been printed; that the words are being newly created from   ≬
≬ your own mind and imagination. Yet the words must also have the   ≬
≬ speed of thought appropriate to the character and the immediate   ≬
  situation.
≈ ≈ ≈ ≈ ≈ ≈ ≈ ≈ ≈ ≈ ≈ ≈ ≈ ≈ ≈ ≈ ≈ ≈ ≈ ≈

VERBAL DYNAMICS

Vital words suggest through sound their weight, movement, texture or emotion. We associate certain consonants with certain impacts and if we fail to give those consonants their precise impact in articulation, we destroy the power of the word.

For example most words beginning with the plosive 'p' sound travel firmly forward after the concentrated pressure and power of the initial letter:

power, pull, push, put, propel, plunge, pour, plough, press, pump, pick, print, point, pedal, pack.

In all these words the lips must have firm central forward movement. Pressure and release will vary to create the exact onomatopoeia of the word – i.e. the lips will press, pout or part in varying degrees. For some words with the initial 'p' the lips will hardly touch and will part gently.

e.g. puff, pale, palpable, pallid, pure, petal, poetry, paper, pollen.

Take words from the first group and synchronise movement as you say the word aloud. Then examine the exact relationship of the consonants and vowels, e.g.:

<u>Press</u>	Perhaps the hand or iron touched the object on	P
	Initiated movement over a crumpled surface on	R
	Travelled through space	E
	Slid along the material with much restistance on	S
		S
<u>Pull</u>	The hand seized the object on	P
	Brought it forward through space on	U
	Felt resistance but movement on the continuant consonant	L
		L
<u>Plunge</u>	Almost one feels two hands are needed for the impetus of	P with L
	The initial action is quickened because of the lurch of the	L
	A quick heavy downward movement seems to be suggested on the	U
	And travel continues without any obstacle on the continuant nasal	N
	An impact is made but not on a fixed obstacle, the water itself or sand or mud may spread but there is still movement on the continuant	GE

Now examine words where the 'p' sound is placed in the final position:
leap, drip, drape, lump, limp, strip, lop, flop, slap, slump, jump.

Notice the tendency of the vowel to move towards the ground to the final 'plop' of arrival on 'p'. Every vowel in these words suggests different spatial travel; there is an arc of movement in 'leap'; a perpendicular descent in 'drip' and extended curve down in 'drape'. Notice how movement changes in direction in 'jump' where the 'm' shows the arrival after descent and the 'p' the resultant rebound.

The sound 'b' in the English language can, in its full plosive quality, be a belligerent and blasphemous sound.

batter, build, break, bend, bore, bash, bull, beat, bark, blood, boom, budge, buckle, burden, boulder, bind, bound, boil, bugle, blare, boor, bounce, bold, bitch, bungle, blast.

Try out the experiments of movement and sound association which you did for its consonantal partner (P unvoiced B voiced).

Bend		
	The object is grasped on	B
	The two hands press through space on	E
	Movement continues slowly with more difficulty because of the resistance of	N
	It comes to a stop of complete resistance on	D

Notice too, the different spatial travel of the vowel sounds; the expansive spread of the 'or' sound in 'broad', the concentric movement suggested in the 'ine' sound of 'bind', the arc movement of the 'oh' in 'boulder', the circulating movement of the 'oy' in 'boil', the flaring movement of the 'air' in 'blare' etc.

In all the above words the pressure of the lips is strong and the plosion loud and sudden but if the lips are lightly and softly parted the sound takes on a palpable beauty and beneficence.

e.g. beauty, bluebell, bud, burgeon, blessing, bounty, boon, blossom, bonny, bairn.

The sound 't' has clear-cut attacking qualities:

e.g. tear, tip, tilt, tap, target, top, took, twist, twirl, turn.

In the final position it suggests a sudden stopping of movement and arrival at a clearly defined terminus:

e.g. hit, hat, bit, bat, cut, shut, shot, sit, get, bolt, lift, drift, cleft, weight, knot, pelt, blunt.

Cut	An instrument is brought in action and grasped on	C
	There is movement of incision on the	U
	The action is complete, a terminus reached on the	T
Weight	Compression and heaviness are suggested in the	W
	Immediately combined with the vowel there is a	
	heavy downward movement on	EIGH
	The scales or object have reached a terminus on	T
Drift	There is usually a brake in movement on	D
	But there is a slow ripple of movement when it is	
	combined with	R
	But it lifts away from the ground on the	I
	And floats in the air on	F
	Then finds an obstacle against which the matter	
	forms a pile on	T

How air-borne the letter 'f' is:

e.g. feather, free, fantasy, fly, fanfarronade, flutter, flare, fan, flow, fluid, falcon, flame, flake, foam, flute, flick, flute, fairy.

But what power against the air we hear in:
force, forge, freeze, fury, fuss, full, foul, fall, fling, flee, flow

when the teeth pressure and breath is increased.

The 's' sound suggests smooth, liquid qualities:

e.g. slip, slide, slope, slush, slender, sink, squirm, squash, sail, sea, sand, sauce, scrub, sift, silk, silver, siphon, sinuous, skid, slash, sleek, sling, sluice, smash, squirt.

In the 'sh' sound there is a wider spread of impact:

e.g. shut, push, shake, shave, shear, shine, shove, rush, shore.

Observe the varying pressures and pace in, for example, movement of a door:

shut, close, bang, bolt, lock, fasten, slam, force.

Each word has its own force, precision and timing.

Notice the different time pattern and concentration in all aspects of looking: carry out the degree of visualisation as you say the word:

> look, see, notice, peep, peer, stare, observe, glance, gaze, glare.

The different degrees of weight and pace in words connected with walking:

> walk, step, trudge, march, trip, sprint, stalk, saunter, strut, stride, tread, plod, loiter, meander, toddle, hobble, teeter, waddle.

walk   direct forward impetus of 'w', the forward movement of 'or' and the clearly defined destination of 'k'.

loiter   the less confined movement of the 'l' the curved somewhat aimless spatial travel of 'oi' occasionally distracted and deterred by the letter 't' followed by the vague unfinished neutral vowel.

Now make your own observations and discoveries in words with other consonants. Notice how the additional vowels and consonants in the word change the weight, direction or texture.

All good writers and speakers choose words which have these dynamic qualities: 'blood, sweat, toil and tears' are simple and powerful. It is words such as these which have persisted from Chaucer to Churchill.

This introductory chapter on the vast and fascinating aspect of evocative language is not intended to be either complete or conclusive. It is simply throwing out a few ideas which will stimulate adventure or enquiry. It is also a small tribute to the hundreds of unknown authors who evolved the every-day words of our language little knowing that they had made them immortal.

(For a more detailed analysis and practice of verbal dynamics, especially valuable for drama students, a study of: 'Into the Life of Things' by Burniston and Bell, ESB publications, is recommended.)

SMOOTH JUNCTIONS

"Good English is plain, easy, and smooth in the mouth of an unaffected English Gentleman. A studied and factitious pronunciation, which requires perpetual attention, and imposes perpetual constraint, is exceedingly disgusting. A small intermixture of provincial peculiarities may, perhaps, have an agreeable effect, as the notes of different birds concur in the harmony of the grove, and please more than if they were all exactly alike".

(Dr. Johnson)

CONSONANT JUNCTIONS

When one word finishes with a consonant and is followed by another word of the same or related consonant:

e.g. black coffee; hot tea; white dog; six soldiers; camp-bed; the two junction consonants are made into one with just a slight pressure hold. There should be no release or rebound.

Liaison is as important in English as it is in French for we listen to phrases not to separate words.

Read the following with easy confluence from one word to another but with precision and clarity.

a)   When two Englishmen meet their first talk is of the weather.

b)   When a man is tired of London he is tired of life. (Dr. Johnson).

c)   The man who can dominate a London dinner table can dominate the world. (Wilde)

d)   True wit is nature to advantage dressed
     What oft was thought but ne'er so well expressed. (Pope)

e)   I disapprove of what you say but I will defend to the death your right to say it. (Voltaire)

f)   Errors like straws upon the surface show,
     He who would search for pearls must dive below. (Dryden)

g)   Work banishes those three great evils: boredom, vice and poverty. (Voltaire)

h)   No man is an island entire of itself; every man is a piece of the continent; a part of the main. (Donne)

i)   There are two tragedies in life. One is to lose your heart's desire, the other is to gain it. (Shaw)

VOWEL JUNCTIONS

Avoidance of glottic shock

When words begin with vowels the sound must flow undisturbed on the breath without a jerk of the glottis. This is as important in speech as it is in singing.

Here is a jingle where initial vowels predominate and where, quite often, the preceding word ends with a vowel:

> We are going to Aden by air
> With an aunt who's over eighty,
> And also in our care
> Is an old and rather weighty
> Uncle who's eighty-eight –
> He may be even more
> For he arrived at man's estate
> In eighteen-ninety four

Now in more serious vein:

> I am a part of all that I have met
> Yet all experience is an arch wherethro'
> Gleams that untravelled world, whose margin fades
> For ever and for ever when I move.
> (Tennyson)
> The winds that will be howling at all hours
> And are upgathered now like sleeping flowers;
> For this, for everything, we are out of tune;
> (Wordsworth)

In doing the above exercises aim at a smooth unbroken flow from one vowel to another without any intrusive consonants:

> e.g. We are; not; we/are weyar
> (there is a similar confluence in: 'by air'; 'be even'; 'thy own')

Intrusive R

Where there is an 'r' at the end of one word followed by an initial vowel link the 'r' to it.

> e.g. – Over eighty; for ever; are up-gathered;

> for everything; we are out-of-tune; pure ' nd endless light.

Be careful not to put an intrusive 'r' between vowels:

> What a good id<u>ea it </u>was
> To give our so<u>fa a</u>way
> Its gone to the dram<u>a ac</u>ademy
> For the ope<u>ra I</u>'m doing in May

(The places where you may fall into the trap are underlined thus:

'idea it' not 'idea' 'r' it')

PUTTING IT INTO PRACTICE

DIALECT? REGIONAL SPEECH? ACCENT?

We are short of a suitable word in speech terminology to define regional or off-standard speech. Indeed what is standard English? And what do we mean by 'accent' which in other connotations means 'stress'? The word 'accent' has, through usage, come to mean a certain quality of speech (usually more apparent in vowel sounds than consonants) which reflects a certain rural or provincial quality. Even in this respect we are inconsistent in our criticism. Educated English with a Scots or Irish accent is accepted anywhere but pedants tend to be critical of other regional differences especially of the midland or northern counties.

So it is up to you to decide whether to change any or part of your own pattern of speaking. Remember there is no such thing as natural speech. No-one speaks by instinct. Speech is slowly acquired by imitation. It is an acquired art to speak at all, so if you decide to change you will not be 'unnatural' but merely changing one acquired pattern for another.

This realisation helps us to be more tolerant and understanding, not only about our own speech but everybody else's. If a child hears a pattern of speech from his mother which you think sounds 'affected' you cannot accuse the child, nor indeed the mother, of 'affected speech'. They are both repeating a pattern of speech thay have habitually heard, as you are repeating a pattern of speech most persistently heard in your childhood.

We must be quite clear and logical in our thinking about this. Do we want to preserve a dialect or are we excusing ill-formed speech which confuses or distracts the listener? Again there is confusion, for many of those who subscribe to the idea of preserving dialect send their children to schools where they will probably only hear the dialects of Mayfair.

Socially, or professionally, 'off-standard' speech may be a handicap. If your work is at executive level, or if you are in one of the learned professions, an 'off-standard' accent may cause doors to be closed on you. They will never even open if you are 'genteel' and adopt a pseudo refined accent. But if you are an actor then you must train your ear and speech mechanism for a range of accents.

Fine shades of differences of vowel sounds are not discernible by the speaker himself. Any correction needs a good teacher who is both patient and exacting and a speaker with infinite self-criticism and will-power. A tape-recorder is useful if used with the guidance and criticism of a knowledgeable tutor, otherwise it can be disheartening or a waste of time.

The following exercises in jingle form on each of the 24 vowel sounds are for those who need more perfection in vowel shaping.

You may not need them at all. Your tutor will guide you in this respect.

Mere repetition is of no value, for if the vowel is being repeated with its original faulty placing, the inaccuracy is simply being more firmly established.

Remember that lips play only a small part in the making of vowel sounds.

Vowels are made through changing the shape of the primary resonator, the mouth. This is done by relaxing the jaw, opening the back of the mouth and changing the tongue shape and position.

However, as vowels are the 'carriers of tone', correction may come fairly easily through aural perception and oral imitation, but the habitual muscular movement of the tongue is difficult to change for some people and they then need to know why they are not changing the acoustic property of the vowel when they think they are imitating the one heard.

Drama students will, of course, be working on many accents and dialects and therefore need acute oral perception and heightened agility of the speech muscles.

General hints for vowel toning:

1) Have a space of at least half-an-inch between the teeth.

2) Keep the tongue tip down out of the way.

3) Avoid spreading the lips horizontally beyond a neutral position.

4) Encourage the forward projection of vowel sounds by releasing the lips from the teeth. Most people suffer from 'stiff upper lip'.

5) Do not allow vowel sounds to go down the nose, unless it is deliberate nasalisation appropriate to the regional or social speech you are adopting.

6) There should be no strain on the layrnx or throat muscles and no glottic shock in initiating the vowel sound.

| EE | (Column 1 in the vowel chart)

Neutral lips, at least half-an-inch space between the teeth. Body of the tongue high in the mouth. Tongue tip down behind bottom teeth. One constant sound with no lip or tongue movement change.

(Spelt: e ee ea ie ei eo ey uay e-e)

When greedy Eve in Eden
Seized fruit from off the tree
And wheedled heedless Adam
To yield and eat, and he
Weakened to her entreaties
And ate with fiendish glee,
She needed to have heeded
The sequel to her spree.

(Speakers with Northern accents tend to harden and tighten this sound to 'eey'. Some Midland speakers precede it with a neutral vowel and change the quality of this single vowel).

| ĭ | (Column 2 in the vowel chart)

As for the EE sound with the arch of the tongue a little lower. The sound is much shorter in duration. French students for example tend to make the sound too much like EE and confuse 'beach' with 'bitch'!

(Spelt: i or e or y)

1) The village of Lymm has a vicar
Whose delivery gets quicker and quicker.
When he visits the sickly
He goes just as quickly
And christening's done in a flicker.

2) Ibsen dismissed from the theatre, villains, princesses,
and heroines. Instead he instituted realism,
intelligence and inhibitions, and in so doing,
filled the auditorium with the intellectual middle class.

| ĕ | (Column 3 in the vowel chart)

Tongue tip down, tongue a little further away from the palate than 'i'. Lips in soft neutral circle. Avoid lip spread.

(Spelt: e a ei eo ea)

1) A lady M.P. who claims to be credible
Says an egg in a shell is never quite edible.
Whether it's fresh or whether it's – well a ....
It carries germs which are called salmonella.

2) "The next question", the Reverend Edgar Fenton said querulously,
"Is whether the weather vane is to be left so perilously,
Suspended on the edge of the parapet, unmended.
When I ask for any money to be spent, the treasurer is offended.
Any-one would think that in expressing a request for a miscellany
Of necessary repairs to be executed, I was committing a felony".

| ă | (Column 4 in the vowel chart)

This vowel is very near to the ĕ sound. Middle of tongue is nearly, but not quite, as high; lips left in the soft neutral circle. Northern speakers tend to make this sound low in the mouth and further away from ĕ. This shift to a flatter ă is noticeable in younger people of all classes and professions.

(Spelt: a only)

It is a good idea to proceed from the ĕ to the ă in practice. e.g. bed, bad; head, had; said, sad; lend, land; to show the subtle, or more obvious, difference.

A fat old man from Zanzibar
Sat on a barrel of coal black tar,
With his hat on his head,
And his hand on his cat,
And his cat on his lap,
He sat with a slap
Bang in the barrel of coal black tar,
So he'll never get back to Zanzibar.

(Drama students playing pre war or older characters may need to adjust this vowel from the current one)

| AH | (Column 5 in the vowel chart)

This is the most open vowel sound. The tongue lies low down in the mouth and the soft palate is lifted high. Bring the vowel well forward and do not allow sound to go down the nose. AH sound is marked in bold print. (Received pronunciation). Many words in the North which in R.P. are pronounced AH keep the ă sound, Practice this with the R.P. 'ah' for jaw relaxation.

(Spelt: ah ar a er)

1) It can't be Great **Aunt** B**ar**bara,
Seen d**a**ncing in the d**ar**k,
It can't be Great **Aunt** B**ar**bara,
Cha-cha-ing in the p**ar**k,
It h**ar**dly could be B**ar**bara,
Who **a**sked the bookie's cl**er**k

If the **Shah** and **Ma**ha**rajah**
Would be racing at Hurst **Park**.
And I **har**dly think that **Bar**bara,
With her **heart** still in the past,
Would drive a **car** to **Der**byshire
So **star**tlingly **fast**.
Through **Berk**shire on to **Hert**fordshire
In a **scar**let Jaguar
Oh **dar**ling Great **Aunt Barbara**
What a **charming aunt** you **are!**

Now practise moving quickly from ă to AH:

2)   Fancy asking Alice to dance
      To that brass-band in the stand.
      She'd rather chat on a grassy bank
      With a brandy glass in her hand.

   In northern English and other variants, e.g.: American, the open AH
sound might not be used in words like aunt, past, glass, etc. This rhyme
too is a good jaw relaxer, so use it in this way as an exercise even if your
native speech rejects this sound.

ŏ   (Column 6 in the vowel chart)

   Make the lips into a firm (but not pinched) circle, the tongue is left in a
fairly neutral position. Send the sound forward and central.

   (Spelt: 'o'. After 'w' 'a' as in wasp, watch (wŏsp; wŏtch)

It's odd about the Morrisons,
They're lost in foreign lands,
They wanted a tropical holiday
On Continental strands.
They watched the foreign adverts,
And totted up the cost
And vanished last October
From our winter fogs and frost.
Oh, they haven't gone to Florence,
To Scotland, or Hong Kong,
But on jolly tropic coral isles
They wander all day long.

| AW | (Column 7 in the vowel chart)

Lips well forward in a firm (but not pinched) circle – half-inch space between the teeth. Send the sound well forward. Modern received pronunciation shows no difference between 'aw' and 'or' (e.g. paw, pore). This may be rather regrettable. Scots and Irish are advised to keep their R sound. English people please use the R in liaison with the following vowels (e.g. more and more).

(Spelt: aw au or ore)

1) Naughty St. Audrey
    Has brought us the word 'tawdry'
    For she always bought baubles
    And trinkets that were gaudy;
    Our language would be short
    Of a word of that sort
    If Audrey had been haughtier
    Instead of being naughtier.

2) One gaudy night in Marlborough (NB Mawlbra)
    A gorgeous courtesan
    Walked down the hall
    With light foot-fall
    Her face behind her fan.
    At dawn of morn in Marlborough
    A courtier quickly ran
    Towards the lawn
    With sword out-drawn
    And caught and fought her man.

(Notice salt, malt, Marlborough all with 'aw' sound. 'Off' is pronounced 'awf' by many southerners and is given the first place by Daniel Jones in his Pronouncing Dictionary. Nowadays it sounds old fashioned or cockney or affected).

| oŏ | (Column 8 in the vowel chart)

Tongue tip down. Lips drawn into a soft circle. Be careful that you are not confusing it with the ŭ sound of 'hut' or the 'o͞o' sound of 'moon'.

(Spelt: oo u o)

Cook, book, good, hook, look, push, put, pulpit, cushion, sugar, butcher, buffet

Sebastian the bull, sooty-black bull,
Looked at the bull-ring – the arena was full;
And he just wouldn't put inside it one foot!
It was no good the Picadors, woolly-clad Matadors
Pulling and pushing and slyly ambushing –
Sebastian just stood like a bull made of wood.
Then the matador took his red cloak out and shook –
See! The Picadors push on a red woollen cushion
But Sebastian the bull thought "I'll pull the wool
Right over their eyes! I'll hoodwink the guys!
Their red cushions and cloaks couldn't cook up a hoax.
Why on earth should I mind for I'm quite colour-blind!"

| oo | (Column 9 in the vowel chart)

Lips well forward in a small firm circle. Tongue tip down and jaw relaxed. Sides of tongue pressing against the upper teeth so that the tongue forms a hollow groove. When this sound is out of true (e.g. in many regional accents) the single vowel is not sustained but is given a dipthongal quality.

(Spelt; oo ou o-e o u u-e)

1)   There was a young man from Permootah,
        Who flew into church on a scooter,
        But the Dean kept quite cool
        And soon made a rule;
        If you scoot on a tomb – sound your hooter!

The New Help Speaks

2)   "I haven't a clue how to do out a room
        Please don't let me loose with a Hoover,
        Do you use spoons for fruit or are they for soup?
        I'll leave them for you to manoeuvre.

        You'd better move Judy, she seems very moody,
        She chewed and then blew out her food,
        Oh, no I refuse to clean all the shoes,
        (There's Judy again being rude!)

        As a rule where I'm working the kids are at school,
        And I'm not asked to do work that's dirty,
        So I'll soothe my bad nerves if you'll pass me a stool
        And see who has won the 'two-thirty'.

For ear training try it again with a regional 'oo' sound and then a standard one. A Birmingham accent would suit this rhyme!

| ə |

THE NEUTRAL VOWEL (Column 10 in the vowel chart)

The flexibility and pleasing cadences of the English language depend very much on the neutral vowel. This sound occurs in every possible position and is spelt in innumerable ways. Moreover the subtle change of meaning of a sentence can be precisely determined by the degree of neutralisation of certain words. If we make a plain statement of fact, for example, and say: 'He was a good man', we neutralise the 'woz' to 'wəz'. If his goodness has been questioned we might say: 'He was (wòz) a good man'.

In the easy coloquial speech of a well educated and well adjusted person this vowel makes a valuable contribution to the rhythm of speech. A tiring and clumsy syllabic stress is avoided. This is extremely important in the teaching of spoken English to E.A.L. students for the spelling may be: a e u o io ou ir oi ai ough er ar ur, all representing the neutral vowel.

In verse-speaking and drama the neutral vowel is significant in determining rhythm and pace.

(See section on Metre and Rhythm. Page 56)

| ŭ | (Column 11 in the vowel chart)

1) The constables hurry from London
    Chasing culprits who're out on the run,
    The thugs are not rough
    For with cunning and bluff
    They've posed as a monk and a nun!

Distinguish between ŭ and oŏ (the oŏ sounds are underlined)

2) Just as the church clock struck, 'One!' my cousin looked and saw a
    bull running towards the mulberry bush. On an impulse he took a
    sudden lunge in the bull's direction which just as suddenly stood
    stock still under the mulberry bush. The parson hearing the bull's
    full-blooded roar rushed from the pulpit and instructed the unlucky
    butcher who had lost the bull to pull it away from the mulberry bush
    into safe custody. No wonder my cousin who had impulsively run to
    the mulberry bush felt a flutter of his pulse as he helped the butcher
    to pull the bull towards the hut. Meanwhile the parson, feeling
    unable to return to the pulpit said he would go back to his study.
    After shutting the study door he subsided on the nearest cushion
    feeling that he was suffering from severe concussion.

$\boxed{\text{ER}}$ (Column 12 in the vowel chart)

Relax the jaw. Lips away from the teeth. Tongue in relaxed position.

(Spelt: er ur or ir our eur ear yr)

1) Sir Ernest Hearn's a connoisseur
Who does research on churches,
An amateur, who does prefer
The clergy for researches.
From early youth right from his birth
(This from his nurse I learn)
He worked and worked with little mirth
And spurned the urge to earn!

2) 'The early bird catches the worm'.
The proverb always makes me squirm.
The early earth-worm stirring first
Does not deserve to be so cursed!

$\boxed{\text{OH}}$ (Column 13 in the vowel chart)

Relax the jaw, lips in soft circle well forward. The vowel has a diphthongal quality. From the position of ŏ it moves quickly to oŏ. This vowel is distorted by many people in various parts of England, not least in the west end of London. Listen for a pure 'round' vowel and resist the present tendency to make it ĕ oo or ay oo.

(Spelt: o oa ou o-e eau oo ow ew eo)

Epitaph for our Gardener

1) Here reposes Joseph Moses,
Where he's gone we do not know.
Perhaps in heaven he hoses roses
As he hopes we do below

2) In Shrewsbury lives a yeoman
Who mows and hoes, and sows
Seeds that were sown in Roman times
Close to the Roman Road,
And as he goes through Shrewsbury
From echoes long ago
He hears the Roman soldiers
From Shrewsbury to Ludlow.

| AY | (Column 14 in the vowel chart)

This diphthong is formed from ĕ and ĭ gliding into one continuous sound. Faulty interpretation of this diphthong arises when another vowel is substituted for one of the components – e.g. ă ĭ or a nasalised AH for the first part of the diphthong. Avoid any horizontal lip spread.

(Spelt: ay ai a-e eigh ei au)

1) My friend Jane Yates has gained in weight
And changed her dainty shape.
She stands on scales
And there bewails
Her hateful shameful state.
Each day at eight,
And never late
She takes her measuring tape
Alas it's plain
Another gain
Her waist's reached thirty-eight.
Weight-Watchers wait for the great day
And they'll record the date
When Jane will say:
'Callooh! Callay!
I've lost eight pounds in weight.

2) 'Gaol' and 'jail' are the same name for the same place

| I | (Column 15 in the vowel chart)

This is a dipthong formed from a sound midway between 'AH' and 'ŭ' and finishing on ĭ. In the North the sound often lacks the open quality in the first element. In the South there is often too much nasalised AH at the beginning of the vowel. In each case glide quickly from the first element to the second. Keep the jaw relaxed.

(Spelt: i ie i-e eye igh eigh ui uy y)

1) My wife sighs at our curate's eyes.
I cannot find their light divine,
For while he prays he closes his
And while he preaches I shut mine!

2) Here lie the bones of Ida White
She took life in her stride,
She neither looked to the left nor right
Ignored the guiding traffic light
I'm not surprised she died!

| OW | (Column 16 in the vowel chart)

This is a diphthong formed from AH and oŏ. Deviation from this sound arises when another vowel is substituted for the AH – e.g.: ĕ. The diphthong lacks tone and finish if the oŏ is not given its round forward quality, but the glide from the AH to the oŏ should be done with diminishing pressure to a gentle finish. This is a very good exercise for forward lip mobility. Avoid any horizontal pull of the lips.

(Spelt: ou ow ough)

1) Oh we are rather proud
Of the Viscount in our county
(Though he may be rather gouty and is now a little stout)
But in the Upper House you never hear him grouse
For he's on the moor or downs
Far away from all the towns
With his grouse.
Or he may be found at Cowes,
On in Cheshire with his cows,
Or at Oundle where he's Master of the Hounds,
Or fishing in Blairgowrie
For the trout who like it showery
But now-a-days he's never
In the House.

Try this rhyme at speed for agile articulation:

2) There's a cry and a shout, and a deuce of a rout,
And nobody seems to know what it's about,
The monks have their pockets all turned inside out.
All turned inside out! All turned inside out!
(The Jackdaw of Rheims)

| OI | (Column 17 in the vowel chart)

This is a diphthong formed from ŏ and ĭ. Again deviation of this sound arises from a substitution of another vowel for the ŏ or the wrong time values in each element.

(Spelt: oy oi)

Roy's employed in Droitwich
In a first-class oyster bar.
Moira tends to loiter
As she sips her Noilly Prat.
How adroit he is, and poised he is
When he disjoints the oyster,
And Moira squirts the lemon juice
To make her oysters moister.

This is a diphthong formed from ĭ and oŏ. Glide quickly from the first element. Be very careful that the i vowel is enunciated especially in words like: Tuesday, tube, tulip, Duke, dew, dune, suit. Think of it as 'yew'.

(Spelt: ew eu iw u-e)

1) The Duke lined up his serfs in queues
   To take from them their feudal dues.
   The serfs called out: "We all refuse
   To pay to you those feudal dues:
   We'll only give you what's your due,
   We've had enough abuse from you!"
   And so the Duke, suspecting mutiny
   Removed from them his feudal scrutiny!

2) Orpheus with his lute
   Was never mute
   So Zeus made an excuse
   – Avoiding abuse –
   And sent Orpheus to view
   Two Gods – rather new –
   One 'Youth', one 'Beauty',
   He must do his duty!
   Orpheus took his cue
   And with his lute flew.

(Note Orphewss, Persewss, Zewss, etc.)

3) I knew it was the skylark's tune
   (He knew I knew he knew)
   He tuned his notes above the dune
   As clear as drops of dew.

(See how delicately you can say the last verse. It is also a good exercise for subtle intonation and stress).

AIR (Column 19 in the vowel chart)

This is a diphthong formed from ĕ and ă Open the mouth well for ĕ the first part of the vowel. Close a little for the neutral ə which follows. Keep the whole diphthong free from 'closure' and 'spreading'. Merseyside folk tend to make this sound 'er'; so if you are acting a Merseyside character try transposing this verse from R.P. to Merseyside.

(Spelt: air ayor are)

1) Our woman Mayor's an heiress
   A lady rare and fair,
   But do not call her Mayoress
   Address her: 'Mr. Mayor'
2) A dancer whose steps are hilarious,
   Just wobbles on points quite precarious.
   And from deep in their chairs
   Her family just stares,
   Relieved that its pleasure's vicarious!

OOR (Column 20 in the vowel chart)

This is a diphthong formed from oŏ and ə. In the following rhyme both 'oor' and 'ure' are used. Notice carefully which are which.

(Spelt oor uhr our ur)

1) The gourmand simply lives to eat,
   The gourmet makes quite sure
   That all his wine and fruit and meat
   Are chosen with 'amour'.
2) On a European tour in the south of the Ruhr
   A curious thing happened to Muriel Moor,
   She's allured by liqueurs – a taste that's luxurious,
   But we were quite sure that the brandy was spurious.
   Muriel, however, assured us: 'It's pure!'
   She's now home in Truro enduring the cure.

N.B. European, curious, Muriel, allured, liqueurs, luxurious, spurious, enduring, cure, URE Column 22).

EAR (Column 21 in the vowel chart)

This is a diphthong formed from ĭ and ə. Avoid a too closed finish to the vowel which gives a suggestion of an intrusive Y 'eeyer', an ugly tight sound. Leave the neutral sound open but not 'ah'.

Vera Sheard who lives near here
Is a little queer, I fear.
She asked the nurse to pierce one ear.
The nurse replied: 'Miss Sheard, my dear,
I do not want to interfere
But have you really made it clear?'
'One ear', said Vera, 'pierce it here,
The other's useless, I can't hear'.
Well this may seem a trifle weird
For Vera Sheard then disappeared
And now we hear she's Lady Sheard,
She's in the House and really Peered
And geared to start her new career
With one clear diamond in one ear!

(Column 22 in the vowel chart)

This is a triphthong formed from ĭ and oŏ and ə. As with the EW vowel be sure that you sound the ĭ at the beginning and open out well for the neutral ending.

1) Muriel deals in miniatures
    At prices quite luxurious,
    Her clients think they're centuries old
    But Muriel knows they're spurious!

2) In January in a Newry Court
    She lured the judge and jury
    To say a 'Durer' she had bought
    For the gallery in Newry.
    A furious expert some weeks later
    Secured redress for the curator.

OUR (Column 23 in the vowel chart)

This is a triphthong formed from AH and oŏ and ə. Open the mouth well for the AH and after the following closer lip-circle of the oŏ relax to the open neutral e. Avoid too tight lip movement on the oŏ or there will be 'w' in it which makes it a hard sound.

1) 'Clang!' from the Tower sounding the hour.
    'Cowards now cover!
    'Boom!' from the Tower sounding the hour.
    'You're in our power!
    You're in our power!'

2) Glendower left his tower on the heights
    And summoned all the power of his knights.
    He rode down with aspect sour
    To make his subjects cower
    But they glowered at Glendower and his knights.

IRE (Column 24 in the vowel chart)

This is a triphthong formed from ă and ĭ and e. Open the mouth well for the ă and move quickly through to ĭ to a relaxed neutral sound. This can easily become nasalised if the tone is not brought well forward. Avoid the prevalent 'ah' sound for this strong triphthong.

1) An Irish squire consumed with ire
    Was asked by the buyer what he'd require.
    'I make no enquiry. Just look in my diary.
    You sent to the priory a dryer so dire
    It's thrown in the mire. You, sir, are the buyer
    Who hired me the dryer saying clothes would be drier
    Than dried by the fire! Well all I require
    Is to say: 'You're a liar!' So now I'll retire to the priory!"

Any correction of vowel sounds depends on perceptive listening to a good speech model. The printed instruction can only guide you towards better shaping. It will be your concentrated and critical listening plus practice to make the sound habitual, and therefore appear 'natural', that alone will give complete conquest. Practise these vowels sounds or those you most need in conjunction with the relevant column of the vowel chart. Remember that you may be trying to undo years of habitual muscular movement and therefore for a time the sound may seem 'unnatural'. In any case aim at good head tone. Don't discard your linguistic ancestry and your home speech. Get to know it. Be yourself, but with a new linguistic dimension and a good ear for R.P. and other dialects.

For further more detailed phonetic and pronunciation study refer to:-

An introduction to the pronunciation of English
    A.C. Gimson (Edward Arnold)

An outline of English photenics
    Daniel Jones (Cambridge, Heffer)

The Phoneme. Its nature and use
    Daniel Jones (Cambridge, Heffer)

English pronouncing dictionary
    Daniel Jones (Dent, Everyman Library)

Vowel Section parts II to IV

Voice production
    Greta Colson (Pitman 1982.)

A Guide to Good English in the 1980's
    Godfrey Howard (Pelham Books)

Pronouncing Dictionary of British Names
    G.M. Miller (B.B.C.)

Longman's Lexicon of Contemporary English
    Tom McArthur (Longman's 1980)

≈ ≈

REMEMBER

that vowels carry the tone, so relax your jaw, keep the tongue-tip down. Have a sensation of 'forwardness' and 'roundness' using the whole of the mouth as the primary resonator. You can then develop the use of the whole head for secondary resonance. Feel the vibration through the skull and the chest.

≈ ≈

CONSONANTS

In the first section of Part II you learnt how to shape the vowel sounds and send them forward in a rounded stream of tone. Consonants break and separate the singing tones of the vowels and therefore give clarity and outline of words.

For clear crisp consonants check that:-

- the tongue-tip is agile

- the central muscles of the lips are mobile and lacking in tension – avoid the English 'stiff upper lip'!

- the lips are never drawn tight nor spread horizontally; they should never stretch beyond the normal mouth position

- tongue and dental sounds are centralised and not spread

- the nasal passages are clear for the 'm' 'n', and 'ng' sounds

Most of the consonants can be paired together into unvoiced and voiced examples of the same formation:

UNVOICED		VOICED
P	←——————→	B
T	←——————→	D
K	←——————→	G (gold)
F	←——————→	V
S	←——————→	Z
SH	←——————→	GE (measure)
CH	←——————→	J (jug)
TH (as in thin)	←——————→	TH (as in then)

Nasal consonants M, N, NG. Any nasal obstruction will impair these sounds. Practise humming to increase nasal resonance.

L	Light	when the tongue-tip touches the front gums and the sound passes through the sides of the tongue, e.g. lake.
	Dark	when the tongue shape assumes a 'low resonance' position with the tongue-tip pulled back e.g. fill.
H	aspirate	This is always followed by a vowel.
W and Y		almost become parts of the vowels with which they associate.
R		a) Fricative b) Flapped c) Rolled

| P | Unvoiced. | | B | Voiced. |

Consider the onomatopoeic qualities (sound conveying sense) when varying pressures are used for the 'P' sound. See the earlier notes on verbal dynamics.

As a strongly exploded initial sound: put, pull, push, power, press, pelt, pack, prick, pound, pout, pedal.

As a lightly pressed initial sound: puff, powder, pale, pure.

The fluid dropping quality when this consonant is in the final position: leap, drip, drop, flop, dip, plop, ripe, drape, drop, limp, mop, slop, slip.

The contempt in the pushed forward plosion of:

'Portions and parcels of the dreadful past ...'   (Tennyson)

The pathos of:

'The pang of all the partings gone
The partings yet to be ...' (Francis Thompson)

The passion of:

'... peevish boys pleading for your passion'.
'... every petty pelting officer'.   *(Measure for Measure)*

| B |

Most consonants have similar pressure variations; use them perceptively to heighten the mood or image in all expressive speech.

Vary the pressure of the B sound and the volume to give the strength of the first three lines and the delicacy of the last in:

Build your bridges bold and bended,
Build your bulwarks' stubborn ranks
Batter down with big bull-dozers
The budding blue-bells on the banks!

| T | Unvoiced. | | D | Voiced. |

This sound should be articulated centrally between the front teeth with as little escape of breath (or saliva!) as possible.

Be careful that final T's are articulated but do not go to the extremes of the 'elocutors' who reduplicate final and initial consonants, e.g. hot tea. In good speech these two consonants are continuous with just an extra pressure for the second sound.

There's quite a lot I'd like to see
From time to time that's on T.V.
But when I'm asked to visit friends,
I do resent the present trends.
Why travel twenty miles away
Only to hear my old friends say:
"Sit down, we thought you'd like to see
Terry Wogan on T.V."
And so we sit, without a bite
Another teeveetotal night!

Consider the onomatopoeic qualities of the T sound; the short decisive attack of:

shot, hit, tap, tilt, bat, trot, cut, twist, trim, tip.

| D |

Be careful not to de-voice final 'd's unless they are attached to an unvoiced consonant, e.g. stepped, dressed; the 'd' becomes 't', but this must not happen in 'cupboards', 'Bradford' etc.

This sentence contains examples of the 'd' in initial, medial and final positions:

> When we feel dragged down to the depths of despair we should consider this good advice; our characters are depicted in our attitude towards adversity; if we stand up to it undaunted it will develop us; if we display fear, it will diminish us.

Consider the onomatopoeic qualities of the sound D. It brakes movement and closes doors: lodged, dam, damper, dead, dud, clod, sod, load, lid.

Coleridge uses this sound most effectively to point the deep despair of the Ancient Mariner:

> The many men, so beautiful!
> And they all dead did lie;
> And a thousand thousand slimy things
> Lived on; and so did I.

| K | Unvoiced. | G | Voiced.

These sounds are formed by the body of the tongue moving away from the palate.

1) He clicked the big black key and closed the lock.
   (notice the onomatopoeia of the K: it suggests closure)
2) The Canon's face was rucked and wrinkled with care.
   (the 'k's here have a contracting quality)
3) As Kathleen closed the cookery book she carelessly knocked the cup of cocoa over the coffee cake.
   (the onomatopoeia of knocking is repeated here in nearly every word).

| G |

Most of the 'g' sounds in the following sentences are hard but in 'language' the second 'g' sound is a 'j'.

> Girls and boys who go to schools where they do not learn grammar cannot grasp the structure of their own language but later may have to grind away at the groundwork of grammar before acquiring a foreign language.

Consider the onomatopoeic qualities of the 'g' sound. It often, suggests a strong, heavy resistance and slow movement: drag, flag, flog, sag, clog, gag, log, nag, plug, brogue, dug, glut, grip, grasp, etc.

F	Unvoiced.		V	Voiced.

This sound presents no difficulties, indeed, it is one that is too often substituted for the 'th' by those acquiring our language. The only difficulty that arises is when it is in conjunction with other consonants, e.g. twelfth.

> Ralph found that he had the twelfth ticket for the raffle. He was less thrilled when he found that the prize was artificial flowers made from fluffy feathers!

Consider the onomatopoeic effect of the 'F' sound when there is light pressure, how air-borne it is: flutter, fly, fairy, lift, drift, fantasy, fountain, fling, flourish, phantom, fan, fan-fare, feather, fire, flash, flare.

But how contemptuous it can be when the sound is articulated with greater force of teeth and lips:

> How futile it is trying to keep this filthy floor clean!

> I don't care a fig for your fine friends!

The vocalising of the F to V adds vibration and depth and a sense of ease and relaxation:

> Vivien loves to wear velvet, veils and velour.

Marlowe and others made repeated use of this letter in:

> Come live with me and be my love
> And we will all the pleasures prove ...

Today he might say:

> And so my love come live with me,
> I've got a car and a T.V.
> So we can sit and never move
> And all the passive pleasures prove!

| S | Unvoiced. | Z | Voiced. |

S. This sound is the narrowest stream of air that can be expelled from the mouth. If the S is faulty it is usually because the tongue-tip projects too far forward (may be through tooth gaps) or the back of the tongue is flattened and the sides spread.

With the sides of the tongue pressed lightly on the upper teeth, send the air through the central meeting place of the front teeth. Keep the lips forward and clear of the teeth. Avoid any over-hissing.

If there is any difficulty with this consonant, practise directing air on to a pencil point held one inch away from the centre of the mouth or send the air between the teeth through a drinking straw.

Sydney Swanson is in the Science Sixth; he says that the subjects he is studying for Advanced General Certificate are physics, chemistry and mathematics.

Be careful that all the consonants are sounded in:

The smugglers risked capsizing the rafts when they stacked sixty casks of sack on to them.

Consider the onomatopoeia of the S sound, the fluid smooth quality in:

sea, slush, sponge, sop, slosh, sink, sizzle, steam, slip.

The smooth polished surface of:

silver, stone, steel, straight, streamlined, slim, slate, silk.

| Z |

This sound, although rarely spelt as Z, occurs very frequently in English words as an S letter.

Who knows if those are hose? The legs are so exposed that only she who rolls on tights and spends pounds and pounds on nylons knows that they are hose!

(11 z sounds in that sentence but spelt S)

Practice the following rhyme to get forward vibration of the voice:

'Buzz' says the bee
As he flies to the posies
Of pansies, lilies, daisies, roses.
'Buzz' says the bee
In the scented tree,
I've been so busy
It's made me dizzy
So lazily he hums and goes
Drowsily home for a cosy dose.

(23 Z sounds in this rhyme)

| SH | Unvoiced. | GE | Voiced. (as in the French 'rouge') |

These sounds present no difficulty but confusion often arises when they occur with S sounds in a sentence.

> When English words derive from French:
> Chalet, chanty, champagne, chic.
> SH is said – the sound in 'drench',
> But K is used if they are Greek.*

*character, chorus, choir, chord, chiropody, chimera, choreography, etc. have Greek derivations and the ch is pronounced K.

| GE | The English spelling of this sound is usually S:

> Leisure without measure
> Is a doubtful pleasure.
> Staring under boughs
> In an enclosure for cows
> In muddy confusion
> Holds no illusion!

When we visit the garage to discuss the automobile's chassis and the beige cellulose for the body-work, we are using words which come from the French.

| CH | Unvoiced. | J | (dge). Voiced. |

The only diffculty that may arise in making this sound is that other consonants which are linked with it may be submerged, e.g., latched.

The preceding T in match, latch, clutch, etc. makes no difference to the sound.

Try this tongue twister quickly:

> A chewit is a chatterer
> Who chatters as he chews,
> When a chatterer chews
> Or a chewit chatters
> What does the chatterer
> Choose to chew?
> What is it the chatterer chews?

Be careful with final consonants in the following:

> The rich Chinese merchant challenged the furniture dealer that the Chippendale chairs he had chosen from those which were sketched were not Chippendale but cheap reproductions.

1) Last June on my European tour, I saw pictures by Giotto (Jotto), Michael Angelo, and the Gioconda (Jaconda) smile of the Mona Lisa by Leonardo da Vinci (Vinchi).

Be careful to articulate the final consonants in:

2) The soldier as he trudged back to his lodgings, felt that his job was hedged about with rejections and injustice.

$\boxed{Th}$ Unvoiced as in 'three'

$\boxed{Th}$ Voiced as in 'then'

There is no difficulty for English people in making this sound although some children substitute an F. Agility of the tongue-tip is necessary for both these 'th' sounds, but there is no need for exaggerated tongue extension; this blurs and thickens the sound.

Thelma and Ruth threw away the thin strips of leather that they stripped off after they had thonged the three pieces together with thick red thread.

The theology tutor was discussing the thesis of a third-year student who had made a thorough study of theosophical and anthroposophical theories.

$\boxed{L}$ (a)   Light, as in 'leaf', 'fly', 'sleep'

$\boxed{L}$ (b)   Dark, as in 'cold', 'full', 'bulge'.

(a) In the first examples (light) the 'L' is formed with the tongue-tip touching the front top teeth and the body of the tongue high.

(b) In the second examples (dark) the 'L' is formed with the tongue-tip on the palate and the body of the tongue dipped.

Notice the rippling fluid quality where 'L' is used.

'I hear lake water lapping in low sounds by the shore'. (Yeats)

Read the following verses. In the first the light 'L' predominates. In the second verse, as the mood changes, there is an effective use of dark 'L's:

Silks and laces for the lady,
Letters from the lady's love,
Laughter ripples through the lattice
As she lifts a long lace glove.

Far away, a dull bell tolling,
Her soldier's lying dead and cold.
She holds the letter in trembling silence,
A crumpled seal; a heart grown old.

[H] aspirate and [WH] (H through a small lip circle.)

The H approximates more to a vowel shape than a consonant but as there is no vocalisation it must be grouped with the consonants.

In old English H was a gutteral sound similar to the Scottish 'loch'.

There are many lively dialects where 'H's are dropped, but this is becoming less frequent.

Some confusion arises from changing fashions; we had, and still have, many words of French derivation where the 'h' is dropped, but words like 'hospital' and 'hotel' have acquired an 'h' in this century. Many of us still prefer 'an 'otel' to 'a hotel' the second; is an awkward liaison.

We still drop the 'h' in: hour, heir, honest, honour, honorarium.

When I see others hammering
A huge hard-headed nail,
They always seem to hit the thing
Direct from head to tail;

But when I hurl the hammer
(However well I've planned)
The nail holds up its haughty head
And I just hit my hand!

In fluid speech where there may be a number of successive H's it is not necessary to sound them in all subordinate words:-

Harry hovered round the Hanover Hotel with his hat in his hand waiting for her to hurry to his side.

(Any or all of 'his' words could have the 'h' dropped without sounding careless or uneducated, in fact to say them all would make the sentence breathy and forced).

[WH]   This is a W sound blown through an H.

It may be asking too much of English people to use the aspirate 'Wh' in words like: when, why, which, where, etc. although it adds a pleasant grace to speech when it is used, as it is by the Scots.

For reasons of onomatopoeia, it should always be used in: whimper, whittle, whine, whip, wheel, whisper, whist, whisk, wheeze, whiff, whirl, whizz, whistle.

$\boxed{W}$ and $\boxed{Y}$

Try moving quickly from the 'W' to the 'Wh' sounds in the following verse. Work for neat central forward lip movement:

What a whale of a whale,
How he whips up his tail
As he whisks up the water to white!
Who can say whether
He'll weather the weather
When he's wheezing away through the night?

This exercise repeated with agility will help to tone up the central lip muscles. Project the lips well FORWARD. Try the verse through first, without voice, as lip exercise.

$\boxed{R}$ a) Fricative   b) Flapped   c) Rolled

a)   Red: the tongue-tip moves forward from the palate to the vowel (fricative)

b)   Iris: the tongue-tip is moved once (flapped or one-tap).

c)   Robbie Burns as said by the Scots (the tongue tip is rolled).

The Scots, Irish and many regional speakers keep a lively R sound in our language. It is regrettable that in modern standard English this sound is often non-existent.

The linking of a final R to a following vowel gives colour and vigour to speech and helps, in many cases, to avoid the staccato jerking of the glottal stop.

four o'clock, far away, Westminster Abbey, here and there, etc.

When there is difficulty in making an R sound, start with a TH (voiced) then draw the tongue in to Z, draw in still further to R.

Repeat this action quickly until the tongue is agile and is able to tilt up to the top of the palate and produce the R.

Try this difficult combination of R's with other consonants:

Ring up the theatrical outfitters, Rose,
They're in the trades' directory;
I must have rubies, ruffles and rings,
Rhinestones, emeralds, red robes for kings
Ric-rac braid and long red hose
And straw for Act Four in the refectory.

Give all the linking R's to the vowels in the following (you may prefer a break after 'larder').

Pour away the jar of vinegar in the larder, it is rather old and has deteriorated.

| M | N | NG | Nasal Consonants

These sounds are formed by obstructing the breath from escaping through the mouth. This barrier is made by

a) the lips for 'm'   b) tongue and palate for 'ng' and 'n'.

In each case the air is directed down the nose.

It is therefore absolutely essential that the nasal passages are quite clear and that the soft palate is actively used to direct sound down the nose instead of through the mouth (if there is blockage of any kind, medical attention should be sought).

With lips touching lightly, but the jaw slightly relaxed, hum any tune. Feel the vibrations coming through the lips and nose.

Practise the following rhyme with full nasal resonance on nasal sounds but be careful not to nasalise non-nasal sounds.

Put your fingers on the upper part of your nose, then on the forehead, move to different parts of the skull; you should feel vibrations through the bones,

> No-one in at 'number nine';
> No-one in at 'ten'
> Not a sound upon the ground
> Of women or of men.
> I stand forlorn, unknowing,
> On this November night,
> When you'll return – or if again,
> You've wandered from my sight.

| NG | The NG is a troublesome sound in many regions. Sometimes the nasal 'ng' is omitted altogether as in the upper class 'huntin', shootin', fishin''. In Lancashire the tongue is often moved before the 'ng' is completed and there is an added 'g' on the palate, 'anything'. The K sound: 'anythin<u>k</u>' can be heard in Cockney speech.

To correct this sound put the tongue firmly on the palate for the 'ng' sounds and keep it there until the sound is completed.

> She sang a song with winging words.
> She sang a song of humming birds.
> She sang and she sang,
> And gaily it rang,
> The song she sang in the morning!

Intrusive consonants

Intrusive R

The people who omit R's that are there, frequently put in R's which are not there. Say the following with easy glide from one vowel to another without putting in an intrusive R

Isn't there a law about diphtheria immunisation?

We saw a new opera in America. I think it may start a new era in music.

Do you like China or Indian tea?

Tessa always goes to Vienna in the Spring.

When Freda attended her first speech class in her drama academy the tutor said that she did not keep her jaw open.

Intrusive T

Many words containing the letters CH are pronounced SH, e.g. drench, lunch, launch, crunch, hunch, munch, punch, etc. Similarly the CE letters together are usually pronounced S

Do not put a T in 'lunch'
It gives you far too much to crunch.
Say 'munch' and 'bunch' without a T,
'Pencil, concert, falsity';
And when you 'waltz' or lightly 'prance'
Let S, not T, flow through your dance!'

Intrusive Y

In some areas where there is tight jaw closure and horizontal lip-spread, e.g. West Yorkshire, there is a tendency to put a Y sound between vowels 'We yar' for 'we are', 'he yis' for 'he is', etc. This can be overcome by relaxing the jaw.

Avoid the glottal stop but why
Put in its place intrusive Y?
'"We are, he is, they ought"', say I
"Can all be said without a Y".

≈ ≈

≀ REMEMBER ≀

≀ No-one who is listening to you can take in what you say if you are ≀
≀ conscious of *how* you are speaking. Vital speech flows in a never- ≀
≀ ending variety of interesting rhythms and cadences sparked off by ≀
≀ the quality of your listening. So don't 'elocute' and don't sound ≀
≀ pedantic. Aim at clarity of consonants without 'explosion'. ≀

≈ ≈

METRE AND RHYTHM

(especially for students of verse-speaking and drama.)

It is outside the scope or purpose of this book to give information or exercises on prosody. It is, however, most important in the interpretation of verse and drama that any speaker has an appreciation of the difference between metre and rhythm.

Metre may be compared with the scaffolding which is erected before creating a building. From it one can see the external size and form; it has an inflexible regularity and rigidity. It gives the initial support. The building will keep within the framework but the framework will be clothed by:-

Rhythm, the building which grows from it. It will never go outside the framework of the scaffolding but its surface and contours are 'filled in' and infinitely varied.

When we have finished a building we take the scaffolding down - so it is with metre.

In verse-speaking and poetic drama, the thought and speech rhythm dominate and the metre is kept in the background. In pop music the metre is consistently dominant and is deliberately emphasised with the beat of the drum.

There is no special virtue in writing poetry in metre, indeed it is a good deal easier to write metric verse than good prose.

We often in everyday life use the regular metric feet of verse forms without even realising we are doing so.

Here is a conversation which includes all the usual verse metres:

Iambic pentameter: The metre used, for example, in Shakespeare's plays and in everyday English.

    Schoolboy: I'm SORry SIR I HAVEn't DONE my PREP.

Trochaic:

    Schoolmaster: GET it DONE toMORrow MORNing.

Anapaest:

    Schoolboy: But my PEN and my BOOK are at HOME in my DESK.

Dactyllic:

    Schoolmaster: HOW can I GET you through 'A' level HISTORY?

                    Schoolboy replies:-

Spondee: — —	DEAR SIR
Pyrrhic: – –	you'll need
Amphibrach: - – -	some PATience.

56

Iambic - the metre: $\cdot$ — $\cdot$ — $\cdot$ — $\cdot$ — $\cdot$ —

     and AT my GATE desPAIR shall LINger STILL
     to LET in DEATH when LOVE and FORtune WILL.

    the rhythm:
       and at my gate des**pair** shall linger still
       to let in **death** when love and fortune <u>will</u>

(Raleigh)

Trochee—the metre: — $\cdot$ — $\cdot$ — $\cdot$ —

     DRAGGED it WITH its ROOTS and FIbres
     FROM the MARgin OF the MEADows

    the rhythm:
       Dragged it with its **roots** 'nd fibres
       from the **mar**gin of the **mead**ow

(Longfellow)

Anapaest—the metre: $\cdot\cdot$ — $\cdot\cdot$ — $\cdot$ — $\cdot\cdot$ —

     and the TENTS were all SILent, the BANners alONE
     the LANces unLIFTed, the TRUMpet unBLOWN.

    the rhythm:
       'nd the **tents** were all **sil**ent, the **ban**ners alone
       the **lan**ces unlifted, the **trum**pet un**blown.**

(Byron)

Dactyl—the metre: — $\ddot{\,}$ — $\ddot{\,}$

     TAKE her up TENderly, LIFT her with CARE
     FASHioned so SLENderly, YOUNG and so FAIR.

    the rhythm:
       Take her up **ten**derly, **lift** her with **care**
       Fashioned so **slen**derly, **young** 'nd so **fair.**

(Hood)

≈ ≈

Rhythm determines pace

   Remember the **more** words which are emphasised in speech the **less** effective will be the emphasis. Go for the key words; run over the subordinate words with a speech tune which in itself suggests the meaning. Play on the key word either with 'compound inflection', i.e. two or three notes for one syllable or with a minute pause before it.

≈ ≈

Avoid mere volume emphasis.

Let the vocal pattern of your speech be a musical score which conveys the sense.

Read the following extracts dismissing the words in small print **very quickly** and 'playing' in various ways the key words of your script. Notice how the iambic pentameter is flexed into speech rhythm.

1.   If you have **tears**, pre**pare** to **shed** them **now**   *(Julius Caesar)*

2.   For **my** part I had rather bear **with** you than **bear** you; yet I should bear no cross if I **did** bear you, for I think you have no **money** in your **purse**
(as You like it)

3.   I left no **ring** with her, what **means** this lady?
         Fortune **forbid** my **outside** have not **charmed** her
    ⎧ She made good **view** of me, indeed so much ⎫
    ⎨ that sure methought her **eyes** had lost her **tongue** ⎬
    ⎩ for she did speak in **starts distractedly**. ⎭
         She **loves** me sure; the cunning of her passion
         invites me in this churlish messenger.
         None of my **lord's ring!** Why he **sent** her none
         I am the **man!** . . .   *(Twelfth Night)*

4.   Notice how much neutralisation contributes to the variety of pace in:

   the fault, dear Brutus, is not in our **stars**
   But in **ourselves** that we are **underlings,**
   Brutus and **Caesar:** what should be in that **Caesar**
   Why should that name be sounded more than **yours?**
   Write them together **yours** is a **fair** a name;
   Sound them, it doth become the **mouth** as **well;**
   Weigh them, it is as **heavy, conjure** with them,
   Brutus will start a **spirit** as soon as **Caesar.**

(Julius Caesar)

≈ ≈

REMEMBER

If you are studying drama you will find many examples of how the sense-rhythm subscribes to the musical rhythm and determines pace. Notice how the neutral vowel also contributes to the fluent rhythm of verse and prose.

≈ ≈

Notice how very FEW words need a full stress and how frequently in English the neutral vowel occurs.

TEMPO is the over-all rate of a play, act or scene, the time signature, as it were, of the verbal score.

But a play could be produced to keep the intended tempo and yet seem to be dull or slow. The PACE is wrong.

If a man takes three hours to drive from London to Canterbury, that is the Tempo. Whether he stops for lunch; how he speeds on an open stretch of road or how he slows-down for traffic on points of interest: that is the

PACE.

Pace allows for rapid acceleration of whole lines or phrases.

Pace needs fluid and intelligent use of the neutral vowel.

Pace allows for PAUSE and interesting pointing and timing of key words.

It does not mean 'gabble'.

REMEMBER

that Pace in dramatic dialogue, or prose and verse readings, is distribution of stress. Tempo is the overall timing.

Pace is the translation of thought pattern into silence and sound from imaginative thinking. Pace includes a range of speeds.

VOWEL CHART

VOWEL CHART

PURE VOWELS: a single movement

1	2	3	4	5	6
	ĭ	ĕ	ă		ŏ
EE	ĭ	ĕ	ă	AH	ŏ
beam	bid	any	ant	almond	bobbin
beat	built	bed	apple	alms	broth
beef	cylinder	bend	azure	arm	cob
beetle	dish	bury	back	artist	cod
breathe	ditch	cellar	badge	aunt	coffin
breeze	elision	cerebral	cab	bark	cloth
brief	evaporate	deaf	canter	bath	cognisant
ceiling	fig	death	dabble	Berkshire	collect
centenary	fitting	debt	dandle	can't	(noun)
conceive	flick	edge	dazzle	card	controversy
dealer	gymnastics	edible	fad	castle	doctor
deceive	hill	egg	fancy	clerk	dodge
eagle	history	excellent	flag	dance	dog
east	ill	feather	gas	dark	doll
eel	jingle	fetch	gash	darn	flock
epoch	kitchen	fetish	gather	draught	flog
fatigue	limp	gender	hammer	Derby	floss
feeble	live (verb)	generic	hand	demand	golf
field	lyric	get	hatch	far	gone
fleeting	mission	heather	have	farce	halt
freeze	mystery	heifer	jam	father	hobble
heath	nibble	irrevocable	jasmine	garden	jog
heave	pith	jealous	lass	garland	joggle
jeep	quince	jeopardy	lather (or 5)	glass	jostle
keen	relax	keg	Mall	guard	lobster
league	ring	leather	man	half	lofty
leek	sing	led	map	harm	mob
leash	spin	leisure	marry	harp	mock
least	swing	lest	mass	heart	moth
meal	sympathy	lieutenant	nap	Hertford	nod
meek	syrup	many	pastel	jargon	notch
niece	tryst	measure	plaid	larch	polish
peace	twist	medal	plait	larder	quadrangle
penal	village	mesh	prattle	laugh	quality
people	width	miscellany	quack	marble	quantity
plead	women	neck	rabble	mark	quarrel
quay	Yvonne	nest	rash	master	rob
queen	zinc	never	rattle	nasty	rock
reed	zither	next	saddle	pardon	rod
seen	the final	pebble	satchel	park	sob
seat	syllable in:	pedal	shall	parse	scallop
seizure	toffees	pedlar	sham	part	squad
shield	roses	pelt	span	pass	squalid
sleeves	faces	pleasure	stab	qualms	squander
teach	boxes	querulous	stand	rather	swallow
teazle	cases	question	tablet	sample	topple
treacle	doses	red	tackle	shark	tossed
vehicle	gazes	rest	tassle	sharp	trod
weaned	houses	reverent	thank	sparkle	vodka
yeast	mated	send	wrap	startle	voluble
yield	fitted	temper	yap	target	wad
zebra (or 3)	college	treasure		tart	wash
		vessel		trance	wasp
		veterinary		Tzar	watch
		well		vase	what
		yesterday		vast	yacht
		zebra (or 1)		yard	yonder

VOWEL CHART

			TRIPHTHONGS: 3 Movements		
19	20	21	22	23	24
(3 + 10) AIR	(8 + 10) OOR	(2 + 10) EAR	(2 + 8 + 10) URE	(5 + 8 + 10) OUR	(4 + 2 + 10) IRE
air	adjure	beer	accurate	bower	admire
bairn	assure	bier	allure	coward	aspire
bare	boor	cheer	bureau	cower	buyer
bear	contour	clear	capturing	dower	byre
beware	detour	clearly	century	devour	choir
care	dour	dear	curable	embower	desire
chair	Drury	dearly	cure	empower	diary
dare	ensure	diptheria	curing	flour	dire
despair	gourmand	dreary	curious	flower	dyer
fair	gourmet	eerie	durable	flowereth	empire
fairly	jury	ethereal	during	glower	enquire
fairy	luxurious	fear	endure	hour	entire
fare	moor	funereal	endureth	hourly	esquire
flair	moored	gear	Eurasian	our	fiery
flare	mooring	hear	Europe	power	flyer
glare	pleurisy	here	furious	scour	friar
hair	plural	imperial	fury	scoured	Fryer
hare	poor	interfere	immure	shower	higher
(h)eir	poorer	jeer	inured	showery	hire
(h)eiress	poorly	leer	judicature	sour	ire
lair	Ruhr	material	legislature	tower	Isaiah
malaria	spoor	mere	liqueur		iron
mare	sure	ministerial	literature		ironed
mayor	tour	near	lure		liar
nefarious	touring	nearly	lured		lyre
pair	tournament	peer	luxurious		mire
pear	tourniquet	persevere	miniature		pliers
prairie	tours	pier	mural		prior
precarious	Truro	pierce	Muriel		pyre
proletariat	Zurich	queer	pure		quire
rare		rear	purely		require
scarcely		revere	purer		shire
scare		severe	purest		sire
seafaring		sheer	secure		spire
share		sincere	spurious		tire
spare		spear	tureen		tiring
square		tear	Ure		transpire
stair		theatre			tyre
stare		Vera			umpire
tares		weir			wire
tear		weird			
vicarious		year			
wares		Zero			
wear					
where					

This chart shows every possible spelling variant of the particular vowel sound with every related consonant.